The Feather Book

Karen O'Connor

DILLON PRESS, INC.
Minneapolis, Minnesota 55415

Acknowledgments

The author wishes to thank John Walters and Alice DeBolt of the National Audubon Society of San Diego, and the Ornithology Department of the Museum of Natural History, San Diego.

Photos have been provided for use by Gerry Ellis/Ellis Wildlife Collection; Steven Holt, Doug Wechsler/VIREO; Chris Koppie, David Hall/U.S. Fish and Wildlife Department; Thomas A.D. Slager; William E. Black; and Phillip Roullard. Cover photo by Phillip Roullard.

Library of Congress Cataloging-in-Publication Data

O'Connor, Karen.
　The Feather Book / by Karen O'Connor.
　　p.　cm.
　Includes bibliographical references.
　Summary: Describes the appearance, function, types, coloring, formation and structure of a feather, and includes information about the origins of feathers.
　ISBN 0-87518-445-6 (lib. bdg.)

　1. Feathers—Juvenile literature. [1. Feathers.]　I. Title.
QL697.026　1990
598.24'7—dc 20　　　　　　　　　　　　　　　　90-2959
　　　　　　　　　　　　　　　　　　　　　　　　　　CIP
　　　　　　　　　　　　　　　　　　　　　　　　　　AC

Dillon Press, Inc., 242 Portland Avenue South
Minneapolis, Minnesota 55415

Printed in the United States of America
1 2 3 4 5 6 7 8 9 10 99 98 97 96 95 94 93 92 91 90

Contents

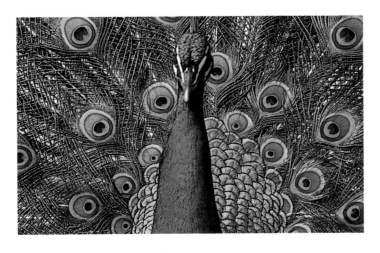

Fast Facts about Feathers

Feather: A feather is one of the light, thin growths that cover a bird's skin and allow the bird to fly

Kinds of Feathers

Flight—Strong, stiff, flexible feathers found on the wings and tail

Contour—Large, fern-shaped feathers that hug the bird's outer body, giving it a rounded appearance

Down—Small, soft feathers hidden beneath the contour feathers as protection against hot and cold weather

Filoplume—Tiny, hair-like feathers found in clusters around the base of some contour feathers

Feather Count

- The ruby-throated hummingbird has 940 feathers
- Most songbirds have between 1,100 and 4,600 feathers
- A bald eagle, though large, has only 7,180 feathers
- A mallard duck has about 12,000 feathers

- Some swans have more than 25,000 feathers
- The tiny hummingbird has more feathers per unit of body weight than the swan
- Penguins have 180 feathers per square inch (28 per square centimeter)

Other Fascinating Facts
- A single wing feather is made up of more than 1 million parts
- Feathers cannot be repaired, but they can be replaced; as old feathers fall out, new ones grow
- Week-old birds have nearly all their feathers— between 3,000 and 4,000—in dozens of sizes, shapes, and colors
- A bird's coloring is one of its best defenses against an enemy's attack
- The feathers of a 9-pound (4-kilogram) bald eagle total 1.25 pounds (.56 kilograms)—more than twice the weight of its bones

 This scarlet macaw displays a set of brilliant red, yellow, green, and blue feathers.

The Fabulous Feather

Feathers are one of nature's most unusual creations. One wing feather has more than a million carefully fitted parts. Not even the detailed workings of a space shuttle can compare to this. Feathers are sturdy, lightweight, useful, and decorative. But feathers are also much more. They protect a bird's skin from injury. They provide a disguise from its enemies. They help birds of the same **species*** recognize each other. And they keep birds warm in cold, wet weather, and cool in the heat of summer.

Yet a feather's most important function is allowing a bird to fly. Without feathers, a bird's wings could not lift it into the air.

*Words in **bold type** are explained in the glossary at the end of this book.

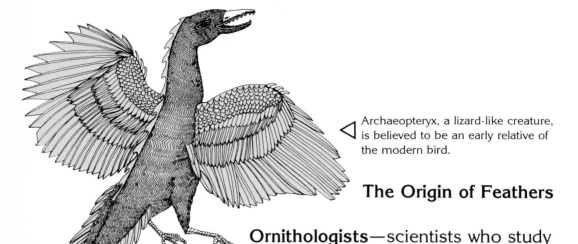

Archaeopteryx, a lizard-like creature, is believed to be an early relative of the modern bird.

The Origin of Feathers

Ornithologists—scientists who study birds—do not know for certain how feathers **evolved**, or developed over time. **Fossils**—the hardened remains of an animal—have helped them trace the origin and growth of some present-day animals by studying the remains of those that lived a million years ago. But with birds, the story is quite different. Fossils have not given scientists any information about how feathers developed.

Scientists do think they know when feathers developed, however. They think that the earliest known relative of the modern bird was a lizard-like creature named **archaeopteryx**, meaning "ancient wing." This unusual animal lived about 130 million years ago, when giant dinosaurs still roamed the earth.

Explorers discovered a fossil of this bird in 1861 in a stone quarry in southern Germany. The fossil shows a creature that is half bird and half reptile, with feathers on its outspread wings. Its **flight feathers** look like those of familiar birds today.

Other fossil research suggests that birds' **ancestors** were reptiles that lived 155 million years ago. Some scientists believe feathers may be a highly developed form of reptilian scales.

Parts of a Feather

Although researchers do not know for certain how feathers evolved, they have studied the parts of a feather and how it grows. A single feather is made up of **keratin**. This dead skin tissue on a typical feather consists of a flat **vane** with a stiff, yet flexible, central **shaft**. The lower part of the shaft is called a **quill**.

Springing from the shaft are fine **filaments**, or threads, called **barbs**. Each barb, in turn, has its own central shaft, which holds even smaller barbs, called **barbules**. At close range, each one appears to be a feather within a feather.

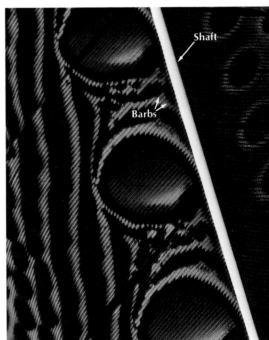

△ Thread-like barbs grow from the central shaft of a typical feather.

9

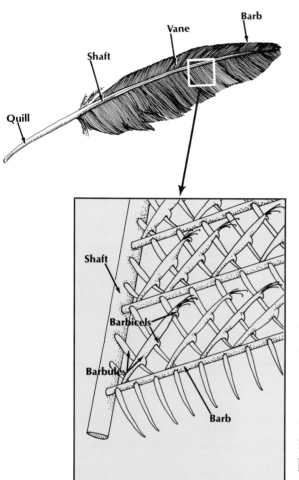

Barb

Vane

Shaft

Quill

Shaft

Barbicels

Barbules

Barb

An enlarged portion of a feather vane. The hooks on the barbicels lock together to form a smooth, flat surface.

A single barb in a crane feather has nearly 600 barbules on each side. This amounts to more than one million barbules in just one feather. The barbules of some feathers are divided even further into **microscopic** objects called **barbicels**, which end in tiny hooks. The hooks lock with the barbicels on either side to form a smooth, flat web that protects the bird from water and air.

A feather begins as a tiny knob, called a **papilla**. It forms beneath the bird's skin. Tightly rolled inside the papilla are the microscopic parts of the feather. This entire structure is set into a **follicle**, or small pocket in the skin. The papilla supplies the color and the necessary nourishment, or food, as the young, undeveloped feather grows.

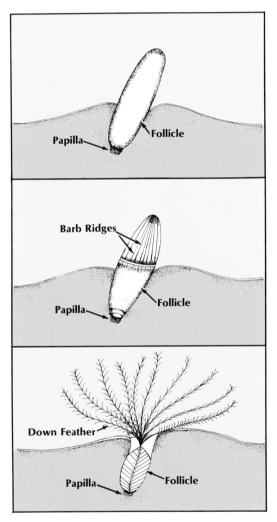

The stages of a growing down feather.

After the feather is fully grown, the blood supply shuts off. From that point on, like human hair and nails, it has no feeling. If a feather is plucked or falls off, the papilla immediately begins to form a new feather in the same follicle.

Kinds of Feathers

Feathers completely cover a bird's body, yet they grow only in certain areas of the skin. Most birds have eight or more pathways, called **tracts**, where the feathers grow. They can be found on the head, down the back, along the sides under the bird's body, on the leading and trailing edges of the wings, around the upper legs, and on the tail. The skin between the tracts is bare, although some birds, such as penguins, are

11

Tertiaries

Secondaries

Primaries

This diagram shows three types of flight feathers.

evenly covered with hundreds of feathers.

There are four common kinds of feathers. Each one has a special purpose. The **contour feather**, shaped some-what like a fern leaf, is the most important and most well known. It is what people think of as a typical feather. The contour has a full-length shaft. The up-per part, called the **rachis**, supports the flat section of the feather known as the **web** or vane. Contours hug the body and give it a firm, rounded appearance.

The flight feather, found on the wings and tail, is one of nature's most perfectly made structures. It is both strong and flexible, yet delicate and light in weight. Thirty to forty of these amazing feathers are all that are needed to support a heavy bird in flight.

The long flight feathers on the edge of the wing are called **primaries**. Of all the feathers, they have the stiffest, most tightly locked vane. The shafts of these feathers, like those of the tail, are thick and strong, and almost straight. They support and move the bird forward in flight. If a primary feather is clipped or plucked, a bird is grounded until it grows a new one.

Smaller flight feathers, called **secondaries**, are located behind the primaries. They are less stiff and have a flexible web. Smaller still are the **tertiaries**, located next to the secondaries, and closest to the bird's body.

The third type of feather is **down**. These bits of fluff are hidden beneath the contour feathers. Most down feathers do not have a stiff central shaft. The silky fibers grow out from a common point. Down is wonderfully soft and light-weight. It forms an excellent layer of **insulation** against cold and hot weather.

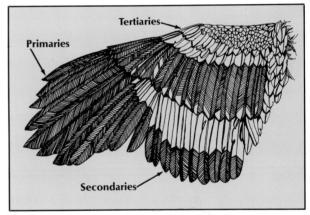

△ This typical wing shows how the feathers are arranged. Tertiaries grow closest to the body, followed by the secondaries and the long, stiff primaries.

Long before people saw the benefits of using down for blankets, jackets, and sleeping bags, birds used it to line their nests and insulate themselves against the heat and cold. The eider duck of Iceland, for example, feathers its nest with down plucked from the female's breast. Herons and bitterns grow clusters,

◁ Down feathers help to insulate a bird's body.

These owls have fluffed up their down feathers, probably in fright. Down also cushions the sound of ▽ flapping wings.

or **tufts**, of down feathers called **powder down**. These feathers grow continuously from the follicle. As the tips of the feathers wear away, they form the powder used to lubricate, or oil, the birds' skin, feathers, and bill.

An under-suit of down also cushions the sound of flapping wings. This allows an owl, for example, to soar silently through the night and swoop down on a scurrying mouse or sparrow.

Fine short hairs called **filoplumes**, usually found on the body of a plucked chicken, are the fourth kind of feather. These thin, bare feather shafts appear in circles at the base of the contour feathers. Ornithologists do not know what purpose they serve.

Another kind of hair-like feather can be found around the bills and eyes of some birds. Once again,

△ Today, in many countries, it is against the law to hunt certain birds for their feathers. Yet in some places birds are still killed so that people may use their feathers. Here, a man wears feathers in a ceremonial headdress, a tradition among his people.

ornithologists do not know the exact purpose of these unusual feathers.

Feather Fascination

Feathers have fascinated people for thousands of years. Unfortunately for many birds, some people think feathers are so beautiful that they have been willing to destroy birds in order to use their feathers.

During the 1800s, for example, the long, graceful plume of the egret was so popular with hatmakers that egrets faced **extinction**—the species was almost completely destroyed. Today, similar problems exist for other species of birds, such as the peregrine falcon and the eskimo curlew.

Until the invention of the metal pen in the early 1800s, people dipped a feather quill in ink and used it as a writing instrument. Today, the quill pen sold in stationery stores is made of metal and is used for decorative lettering.

Several bird protection groups were formed more than one hundred years ago. In 1886, the American Ornithologists' Union formed a committee to protect the birds of North America. The National Audubon Society was a result of this committee. Millions of schoolchildren participate in Audubon study programs each year.

The United States has also

Egrets became endangered in the 19th century when their beautiful white feathers were used to decorate clothing and hats.

approved an agreement with other countries regarding the treatment of **migratory birds**—those that move from one place to another for feeding or breeding. This agreement established laws that regulate or outlaw the trade of rare and endangered birds in the countries that signed the treaty.

The United States Bird Protection Act makes it illegal to take the feathers of any migratory bird, even if the bird is found dead, or if loose feathers are found in the forest or other places. The birds protected under this act include songbirds, hawks, owls, eagles, and vultures.

Both birds and people benefit from these protective laws. Nowhere else in the animal kingdom can one find a more colorful sight than the beautiful wardrobe of feathers that clothe the world's nearly 9,000 species of birds.

The Rufous-backed kingfisher is a tiny
bundle of brightly colored feathers.

Living Color

Feathers come in a rainbow of colors and in a great variety of shapes and designs. They range from the snowy white of an owl in the winter, to the sleek black of a crow. Feathers can be the gray-brown of a sparrow, or the bold red breast of the robin. From the canary's coat of sunny yellow, to the brilliant blue-green train of the peacock, feathers are a bird's most beautiful feature.

Nature's Gift

How does a bird get its color? Where do the stripes, streaks, dots, and bars come from? A bird's colors and patterns result from two situations. The

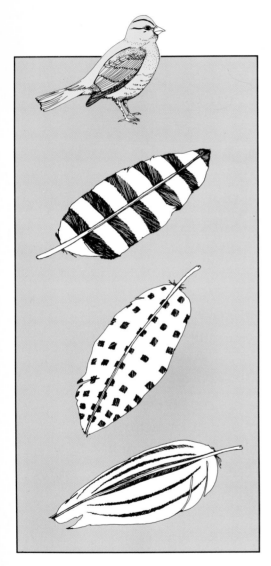

Feathers can be patterned with stripes, dots, or bars, as shown here.

presence or absence of **pigments**—tiny "packages" of color found in the tissues of plants and animals—gives feathers color and pattern. Also, the structure of the feather—the way it is made—causes it to absorb or reflect light. This, too, creates different colors.

In the first situation, a particular color, pattern, or combination of colors is already in place when a bird is hatched. Birds inherit their markings from their parents, just as children inherit blue eyes or brown hair. Only three pigments occur normally in feathers: red, yellow, and brown.

The red pigment produces the bright scarlet color found on a cardinal. A smaller amount of red creates the red of a robin's breast.

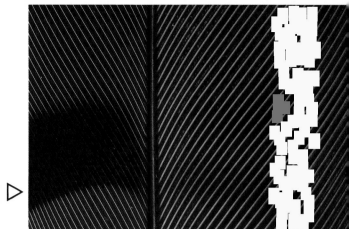

The blue of a blue jay feather is caused when the feather absorbs all light rays except blue. ▷

Large amounts of yellow pigment bring about the bright yellow of a goldfinch or warbler. Red and yellow result in the orange of the oriole.

Brown pigment causes the dull **plumage** of sparrows and thrushes. But in large amounts, it creates the jet black coloring of crows and blackbirds.

Colors other than red, yellow, or brown are the result of the second situation—the way the feather is structured and the way it reflects or absorbs light.

The bright blue feathers of a blue jay or indigo bunting, for example, absorb all the rays of color *except* the blue ones. The blue rays are then reflected, making the bird appear blue.

Some birds, such as the hummingbird and the peacock, present a lovely mix of changing colors. This combination, known as **iridescence**, is the result of a complicated process involving billions of particles of a dark pigment called **melanin.**

Scientists do not know exactly what melanin is made of. But they do know that the particles are arranged in a single layer beneath the surface of the feather barbule. In a peacock or hummingbird, for example, the melanin particles strike the outer surface of the barbule to make iridescent colors. To create the colors of a single peacock feather requires about fifteen thousand melanin particles for every one-eighth inch (.31 centimeters) of feather barb.

Natural Protection

A bird's coloring—however it comes about—is not just something beautiful to look at. It also serves a useful purpose. **Protective coloration**, or **camouflage**, is a bird's best defense. It can often mean the difference between life and death.

Most objects tend to disappear if their coloring blends with the background. Birds are no different. Sparrows, for example, as well as bobwhites and pheasants, spend most of their time on or near the ground. For this reason, their wings, backs, and sides are often colored and marked in ways that look like the bits of grass, twigs, and leaves around them.

Earth-colored feathers also hide female birds from enemies during **incubation**. Their coloring keeps the mother birds safe while warming their eggs and watching over their young after they hatch. When they

crouch low and remain still, it is difficult to see them, even from a short distance.

The brilliantly colored warblers, tanagers, orioles, and rosebreasted grosbeaks, however, would not be safe for a moment in such surroundings. For them, the tropical jungle is the perfect home. If they do fly north, they wait until the flowers and trees are in full bloom. In this way, they can safely blend with their background.

The common goldfinch comes prepared for all seasons. This clever creature changes colors throughout the year. In spring and summer, the male bird wears a suit of brilliant yellow and black feathers. As the leaves begin to turn in autumn, the bird exchanges the yellow coat for green. And by the time the trees have dropped their leaves, the goldfinch is as dull as a sparrow. Its feathers are

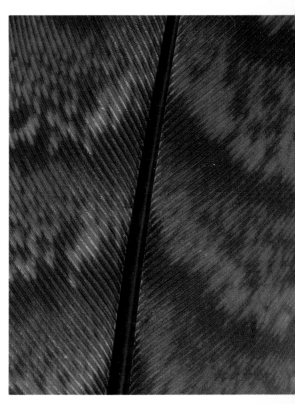

△ The dull brown and gold of the peacock pheasant allow it to hide from its enemies.

23

a mix of dull gray and brown—the same as the bare trees of winter.

Countershading

Some birds are protected by **countershading**. In this common disguise, the bird's feathers are darker on top than on the bottom. Because more light comes from above, the bird appears evenly colored and is less easily seen. Colors and designs that blend with a bird's background help to keep it even better hidden.

For example, the wader's mottled brown and white top side makes this bird look like a pile of pebbles to its **predators**. An owl standing perfectly still may look like the stump of a tree. And a bittern with its beak held high blends in with a field of reeds.

Shorebirds, such as the piping plover with its sand-colored back, and the herring gull with its white underside and gray upper body, blend well with their homes on the sand and sea.

Some birds can confuse their enemies even while flying. The sanderling has a broad, striped pattern on its wings during flight only. When it lands, the bird folds its wings against its body, and the pattern

disappears. Predators watching for the flight pattern might have a hard time locating the "new" bird.

Not all birds rely on protective coloring to remain safe from their enemies. The pure white egret, bright pink flamingo, and sleek black crow are easy to see against their backgrounds. Birds without camouflage usually live in an area with few natural enemies, or they remain alert and keep out of danger. The pigeon, for example, constantly darts its head back and forth as it searches for bits of food. It fluffs its feathers at the slightest hint of danger and is ready to fly off if an enemy appears.

A Colorful Courtship

Many birds use their colors and patterns to attract a mate. Fancy headdresses, broad, colorful tails, and other markings bring males and females together during the breeding season. Male birds may woo their mates by showing off their brightly colored feathers.

The male Mandarin duck looks quite striking at breeding time. He seems to enjoy parading his bright gold whiskers, showy brown and white **crest**—the tuft of feathers on his head—and purple breast. He also displays his glossy green flight feathers, and bold,

△ Iridescent feathers on the peacock provide one of the most fabulous displays of color in the bird kingdom.

orange "sail" feathers along his back. The fashion show comes to an end, though, when mating season is over. At this time, the male Mandarin becomes the same color as the female—the plain brown and gray coloring of a seabird.

The peacock—a male peafowl—can spread the feathers on his back into a beautiful fan that stretches about five times the length of his body. During mating season, the bird parades slowly and grandly in front of the female—the peahen.

Golden and Lady Amherst male pheasants wear feather capes around their necks. Across each feather are bars of black. When the male courts the female, he makes the bars stand up, forming a circle around his head. From the center of this circle peers one watchful eye.

From fluffy neck plumes to boldly colored pennants, from dashing capes to colorful skirts, birds put on one of the most vivid shows on earth.

 A Chilean flamingo preens itself to keep its feathers clean and healthy.

Molting and Preening

Following the breeding season each year, the time comes for birds to exchange old feathers for new. This gradual process, called **molting**, takes about six weeks. It is similar to the shedding of outer layers of skin in snakes and other reptiles.

One Feather at a Time

Most birds go through a **complete molt** in late summer or early fall. New feathers protect them from the cold winter climate, and help them blend with their surroundings. Some birds molt again in the spring. During this **partial molt**, they replace only their worn winter feathers. Old feathers give the bird a drab appearance. This is quite a contrast to the new dress that follows the molting season.

Some species change colors completely. The same bird may be hard to recognize from one season to the next. In its summer plumage, the body of the male scarlet tanager is a fiery red color, with black wings and tail. During the fall molt, however, this bird sheds his bright colors. He takes on a modest coat of olive-green feathers on his upper body, and dull yellow feathers on his underbody.

△ The early molt of this brown booby chick makes it look very different from the adult brown booby.

Some young birds are also difficult to recognize during molting. Their early molts can cause them to look entirely different from their parents. This is especially common among sea gulls and robins. Young gulls look grayish or brownish in color during their early life. Some receive their nearly gray and white feathers the second year.

Other gulls do not get their gray and white adult plumage until they are about four years old.

License to Fly

Flight feathers along the wing and tail, needed to fly, are usually molted less often than the other contour feathers. In most birds, only a few of these flight feathers are replaced at one time. If all the feathers were molted, the bird would lose its ability to fly.

This is not the case with all birds, however. Some birds that spend much of their time in water, such as ducks, geese, and rails, shed their primaries all at once. Then they hide from their enemies for several weeks by swimming, diving, or crouching among the reeds and brush while the new feathers grow in.

These molting chinstrap penguins have large patches of bare skin where their feathers have fallen out.

Feather Care

Caring for thousands of feathers is no small job for birds. Their most basic cleaning habits include **preening**, bathing in water, oiling, and head scratching.

Preening is one of a bird's most important daily chores since a bird's very life depends on its feathers working properly. Preening involves a couple of different tasks. **Nibbling** is the most complete and accurate way to preen. In this method, the bird uses its bill, and sometimes its tongue, to nibble or peck at each feather from the base to the tip.

The second method of preening is called **drawing**. This is similar to nibbling but involves pulling the feather through the bill in one movement. When a bird's feather becomes ruffled or "unlocked," the bird runs its beak down the length of each feather, "zipping" it back into shape. Smooth muscles in the skin also allow the bird to raise its feathers away from the skin in order to clean and rearrange them.

Bathing in water is also an important chore for birds. Water birds bathe differently than land birds. Grebes, for example, have two simple movements. They duck their head and shoulders underwater, then

raise them rapidly in a scooping motion. This sends a splash of water over their backs. They then rub their heads sideways along their folded wings. Some prefer to beat their loosely held wings against the water as it washes over their feathers. Species such as geese and swans sometimes begin their bath with a complete somersault in the water!

The passerine and other land birds usually bathe while standing in shallow water. They lower the front of their bodies and hold their tails clear of the surface of the water. Then they dip their heads and breasts and shake their bills from side to side. Bird bathing may look carefree to a person. Yet it is actually a very organized routine which is carried out by instinct.

Following the bath, a bird will smear its feathers with a fatty substance from the oil gland located behind its tail. The water on its feathers seems to help spread the oil more evenly before it dries and hardens.

When oiling, a bird takes oil from the gland with its bill. Then, with a special stroking motion, it moves the oil to various parts of its plumage.

The oil will help the feathers remain clean and fluffy, and will also keep them from drying out.

◁ This wood duck, like other water birds, is covered with natural oil. This keeps it waterproofed.

Without such a daily "oil bath," birds are more likely to appear dirty and become ill.

Another important method of feather care is head scratching. While standing on one foot, a bird scratches its head with the other foot. Herons and bitterns scratch their heads to clean off fish slime. Passerines use scratching to oil their heads.

Birds take great care to keep their feathers clean and in good working order. But they have little or no defense against human carelessness. In 1989, for example, many birds died from the oil spill in Prince William Sound near Valdez, Alaska. Huge waves of thick crude oil coated or drowned thousands of sea-birds and other ocean creatures.

There is little a bird or rescuer can do in such a situation. The bird's instinct is to clean and straighten its feathers. Yet while doing so, it swallows the oil and dies. Pollution is a bird's most deadly enemy.

Waterproof Gear

The feathers of ducks and other water birds

need more care than most species. A robin or blue jay, for example, would be soaked if it were to jump into a pond. In fact, you can see this for yourself by watching land birds splash in little pools of water on the street or in a birdbath.

Yet a duck is waterproofed with natural oil. A duck can dive into a pond and come up completely dry! Some of the oil is built into the feathers, and some is found in the fat of the skin where the feathers grow. Most of it, though, comes from small oil sacs near the duck's tail.

This waterproof topcoat also keeps the duck warm. Just beneath it is a cozy lining of soft down which covers the lower part of each feather's quill. The skin itself has yet another layer of short fuzz as soft as a young rabbit's fur.

As many as 11,903 feathers have been counted on a mallard duck. No wonder, then, that molting and preening are nearly a full-time job.

These colorful primary feathers are one of the most important types of feathers when flying.

Feathers in Flight

To most birds, flying is a way of life. The key to flying is clean, healthy feathers. The most important feathers for flying are the primaries, the secondaries, and the tertiaries. This thick coat of close-fitting feathers keeps the bird warm and helps it glide easily through the air.

Animals such as bats and insects have developed some ability to fly. But *feathers* have allowed birds to fly in more ways than any other member of the animal kingdom.

Feathers make flying possible because they are lightweight and easily replaced when worn, lost, or damaged. Each feather is also individually attached to

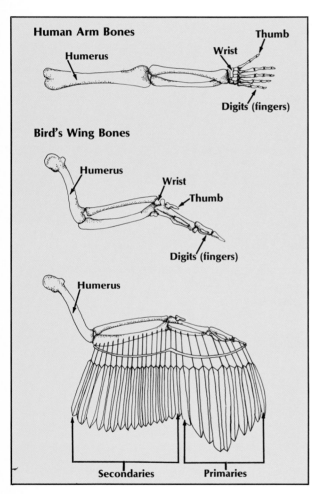

Human Arm Bones
Humerus
Wrist
Thumb
Digits (fingers)

Bird's Wing Bones
Humerus
Wrist
Thumb
Digits (fingers)

Humerus
Secondaries
Primaries

△ A comparison of a human arm and a bird's wing shows how similar they are in structure. Feathers are attached to the bird's "arm" bone.

a muscle that allows the bird to adjust wing and tail feathers in flight. These muscles also make it possible for birds to raise their crest feathers, and open or close body feathers during bathing, preening, and sunning, or for insulation.

Easy as One, Two, Three

The large primaries, or wingtip feathers, grow in the **digits**—finger-like structures—of the wing, and are attached to bones like those in the human forearm. The smaller tertiaries grow in the upper part of the wing. This is called the **humerus**, and is like the area of the human arm between the elbow and shoulder.

38

The shape of feathers is important to different kinds of flight. The wing and tail feathers for one kind of flying might not work for another. Pheasants and quail, for example, beat their wings rapidly to rise into the air, and then they glide off on stiff wings. Their short, rounded wing feathers are not designed for flapping. Like a simple paper airplane, they move quickly for a short distance, then stop.

Up, Up, and Away

In flight, the primary feathers lock together on the downstroke to form a large surface that pushes against the air below. The bird moves forward by pushing the air down and back. If the feathers do not lock together, the bird can lose speed and altitude.

On the upstroke, the wings need to move forward as easily as possible, without fighting the wind. They curve slightly, forming a small surface so air can flow over them easily.

The primary feathers separate on the upstroke, like the slats in a window shutter, so air can pass through the feathers. This cuts down on resistance and makes the wing easier to lift. Then, at the top of the upstroke, the primary feathers lock together, ready

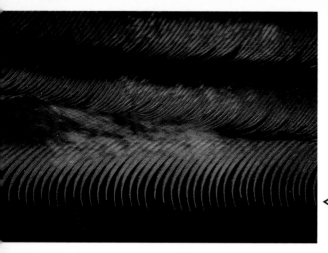

◁ The first primary feather of the great horned owl is fringed for silent flight.

once again for the powerful downstroke.

As a bird flies, it must make some adjustments. It can lower the angle of its wings while facing into the wind to reduce wind resistance. Yet, while doing this, it loses height. If the bird raises the angle of the wings, it will go higher, but slower.

These movements show the importance of preening. Unless each of the thousands of fibers in the feather vanes are zipped tight, the bird would truly be grounded.

Winging It

The feathers on a bird's wing are perfectly arranged to accomplish all these amazing tasks. They even overlap each other from front to back, so the entire surface of the wing stays smooth as the bird soars through the air. When a bird wishes to stop quickly, it can use its wings as a power brake by stroking forward instead of down. It can also stop by turning its shorter wing feathers toward the ground, as a pilot does when she drops the flaps of the airplane's wings.

Different birds use their wing feathers in different ways when they fly. An eagle, for example, has wing feathers that are long and stiff. They are shaped so the air can flow smoothly over the surface of the wing. This allows the eagle to glide for hours without beating its wings.

A pigeon might be called an all-purpose flyer. Its primary feathers act as propellers. The bird's wing span is small, but its flight muscles are extremely large. They let the pigeon flap its wings very quickly.

The tail feathers also have an important function in flying. The shape, size, and length of tails differ among various species. Some are round or forked. Others are pointed or tapered. But all birds that fly use their

△ The wing feathers of the Peregrine falcon are locked tightly together, allowing the bird to glide easily while searching for prey.

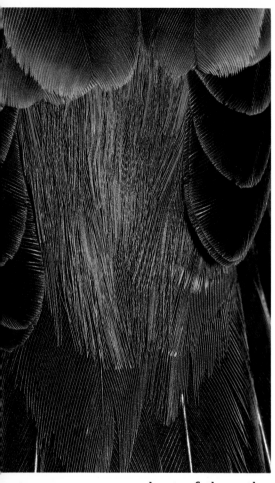

◁ The tail feathers of a blue grosbeak.

tails as a kind of **rudder** to steer and to brake. A bird can spread out its tail feathers like a fan and fold them up just as quickly. Powerful muscles also allow a bird to twist its tail or tilt it, and to turn it up, down, or sideways to help direct its flight. Some species with deeply forked tails, such as terns and swallows, can move each half of their tail independent of the other half.

Humming Helicopters

Hummingbirds and kestrels are sometimes called the "helicopters of the bird world." They are the only species that can **hover** in the air like a helicopter without moving in any direction. The kestrel is also called the windhover because of its ability to rest in midair while searching for food. It faces into the wind and beats its wings while watching the ground for prey.

When the kestrel spots a likely animal for food, it swoops down and grabs it.

Hummingbirds are perhaps the more interesting of these two birds. They, too, can be challenging to watch. This tiny package of feathers usually weighs less than an ounce (less than 28 grams). Unless it perches on a twig or rests on the edge of its nest, the bird watcher cannot see anything but a blur. Most of the time, this little creature is flying about, beating its wings between fifty and two hundred strokes a second.

The ruby-throated hummingbird weighs only a fraction of an ounce, yet it can zip ahead at fifty to sixty miles (80 to 96 kilometers) an hour. Like a helicopter, it can hover in one place. When it is ready to take off

△ Long, thin tail feathers on the blue motmot are used for balance.

again, it can fly straight up, sideways, backward, or forward.

What gives such a small bird so much power? Its feathers do. The wings of a hummingbird are long and narrow, and its feathers are quite stiff. In most hummingbirds, the first primary feather is the longest, and the few secondaries are short. This arrangement and sizing allows the bird to shoot through the air at amazing speeds.

The hummingbird's tail feathers are also important in moving the bird backward and forward, up and down. There are a variety of tail formations, depending on the species. Some groups of tail feathers are scissor-like in appearance. Others are long and pointed. Still others may be forked, squared, or rounded.

Whatever the species, shape, or color, a bird's feathers make the difference. Without them, a

△ The narrow, stiff wings of the hummingbird give it amazing speed.

hummingbird could not hover, and other birds could not fly.

Thanks to the feathers, the wandering albatross can glide on the wind for hours. Feathers also make it possible for the common swift to zip through the sky at more than 100 miles (161 kilometers) an hour. And the arctic tern can fly for more than two days straight without resting—all because of its amazing feathers.

 The head feathers on this crowned crane look like a Fourth of July sparkler!

Fancy and Funny-Looking Feathers

Some feathers are fancy displays of color and arrangement. Others are a funny-looking collection of coarse and hair-like growths that droop from the bird's body like a stringy mop. There are many examples of both throughout the bird kingdom.

The plumage of the peacock is one of the more striking examples of fabulous feathers. The male of the species struts in front of the female during courtship, displaying his colorful wing and tail feathers.

This bird's close relative, the pheasant, is also a lovely sight because of its long, fancy, iridescent tail. The golden and silver pheasants of China and Tibet

◁ The male lyrebird in courtship display.

are known for their remarkable tails. These measure half the length of their bodies. The tail of the Argus pheasant of the Malayan Islands is even longer—nearly twice as long as the bird's body. It also has secondary wing feathers that can grow to three feet.

This species is less brilliant in coloring than other pheasants. Yet its black and light "eye" spots, similar to those of the peacock, create a beautiful accent against the soft grays and browns of the bird's plumage. These unusual markings gave the bird its name. Argus was a hundred-eyed monster in Greek mythology.

The tail feathers of the pheasant are beautiful. But to many bird watchers, nothing can compare to the tail feathers of the lyrebird of Australia. They are among the most unusual in the bird kingdom.

During courtship, the male raises its broad and majestic outermost tail feathers, normally carried low, to attract a mate. For a moment, as they stand two feet (.6 meters) high, the formation of the feathers

resembles a lyre—an ancient, stringed instrument somewhat like a small harp. The lyrebird, about the size of a rooster, cannot fly. Yet it uses its wings when running and leaping.

Kite on the Fly

Yet another collection of fantastic feathers belongs to the rackettail, a species of hummingbird from South America. This tiny bird has a pair of unusually long outermost tail feathers that look like the streamers of a kite. The thin shafts are bare, except for a small group of colorful blue barbs at the tips. These form a racket-shaped vane, giving the bird its name.

Long, ornamental plumes can keep some birds, such as the peacock, from flying. However, if the main tail feathers can still function as a rudder, as they do in the rackettail, then this uncommon plumage is simply an added attraction.

Show of Shows

Perhaps the most majestic bird show is performed during courtship by a group of birds known as birds of paradise. Plumes of every size, shape, color, and texture grow on the male bird's head, neck, breast, **flank**, and back. Australia and nearby New Guinea have forty or more species of birds of paradise. Each bird is more richly decorated than the next. The male magnificent bird of paradise, for ex-

△ A raggiana bird of paradise has long, floating tail feathers nearly twice the length of its body.

ample, has a metallic green bib, a golden cape, and two sleek, curling quills. During courtship, it perches on the branch of a young tree and begins perform-ing. First, the bird points its bill toward the sky, then spreads its cape and fluffs out its glossy green plumes. At the same time, it dances frantically up and down the slender tree branch. One of its relatives, the Prince Rudolph's blue, gains attention by hanging upside down. This causes its wispy, long blue feathers to form a stunning cape.

The male greater bird of paradise crouches on a branch when it is ready to impress a mate. First, it lowers its head

and droops its wings. Then the bird throws up a splash of yellow flank plumes that tumble over its back like a waterfall.

The superb bird of paradise has a fan of velvety black feathers behind its head that springs from its neck. In front rests a bib of glittering, shiny blue throat feathers.

Six shafts resembling stiff wires stick out of the head of the six-wired bird of paradise. Each nearly bare shaft ends in a tiny vane. Breast plumes, spread in a half circle like a ballerina's skirt, complete this unusual outfit.

The seven-inch (18-centimeter) King of Saxony bird of paradise wears an impressive headdress for its small size. Two eighteen-inch (46-centimeter) plumes, deeply notched like the edge of a saw, trail from its head.

Of all the birds of paradise, however, first prize for the best show may go to the twelve-wired bird of paradise. This beautiful creature spreads its six pairs of bright yellow, filmy flank plumes, each one ending with a sharply bent, wiry tip. At the same time, the bird displays a bib of iridescent green and black throat feathers. This beautiful bib completely hides its

◁ An Australian emu.

▽ Close up, emu feathers are dull and shaggy.

head, except for the yellow lining of its wide-open bill.

Funny-Looking Feathers

Not all birds are as beautiful as the birds of paradise. Yet even those of plain plumage are still interesting to watch and study. The five-foot (1.5-meter) tall emu of Australia, and its shy and dangerous cousin, the cassowary, both have odd-looking feathers. Each bird has a massive body—sometimes weighing more than 100 pounds (45 kilograms)—bare and bony legs, a long, skinny neck, and a featherless head.

Brownish-black, bristle-like feathers cover the bodies of these two birds. One bird watcher said they look a bit like long-haired goats with the head of a bird. Neither can fly. The cassowary can be dangerous, though, when using its sharp-clawed toes.

Wing stubs are hidden under the coarse, hanging feathers of the cassowary and emu. Unlike other birds, the feathers do not grow in tracts. Instead, they are scattered over the bird's body, giving it a slightly untidy appearance.

In a sense, all bird feathers are fabulous—even those that are funny looking. No matter what their shape, size, color, or function, each feather is a masterpiece of color and construction. Feathers are the one feature that unites all birds and sets them apart from all other creatures, making them, truly, birds of a feather.

Suggested Reading

Burnie, David. *Bird.* New York: Knopf, 1988.

Cole, Joanna. *A Bird's Body.* New York: Morrow, 1982.

Hirschi, Ron. *What Is A Bird?* New York: Walker & Co., 1987.

Kuchalla, Susan. *Birds.* New York: Troll, 1982.

McGowen, Tom. *Album of Birds.* Chicago: Rand McNally, 1982.

Peterson, Tony. *The Birds.* Alexandria, Virginia: Time-Life, 1980.

Scheffel, Richard L. (Ed.) *ABC's of Nature.* Pleasantville, New York: Reader's Digest Association, 1984.

Wolff, Ashley. *A Year of Birds.* New York: Dodd, Mead, 1984.

Glossary

ancestors (AN·sehs·tuhrs)—distant relatives from whom a person or animal is directly descended

archaeopteryx (ahr·kee·AHP·tuhr·ihks)—"ancient wing"; the earliest known relative of the modern bird

barbicels (BAHR·buh·suhlz)—the end portions of the barbule on a feather

barbs—narrow branches that grow out of each side of the shaft of a feather

barbules (BAHR·byoolz)—miniature growths branching out from each feather barb

camouflage (KAM·uh·flahj)—a disguise used to hide from an enemy

complete molt—the entire shedding of fur or feathers before they are replaced with new growth

contour (KAHN·toor)—a large, fern-shaped feather hugging the bird's body and giving it a rounded appearance

countershading—a type of coloring with parts normally in shadow being light, or parts normally in light being dark

crest—a clump of feathers on a bird's head

digits—fingers or toes

down—a kind of feather; bits of fluff hidden beneath the contour feathers that provide insulation

drawing—a method of preening or cleaning feathers in which the bird pulls each feather through its bill in one movement

evolve—to develop gradually over time

extinction (ehk-STINGK-shun)—the act of wiping out or destroying an animal or plant species so it no longer lives anywhere on earth

filaments—the fine barbs on a down feather

filoplume (FIHL-uh-ploom)—the tiny, hair-like feathers found in clusters around the base of some contour feathers

flank—the lower back area of a bird's body

flight feathers—the strong, stiff, flexible feathers found on the wings and tail

follicle (FAHL-uh-kuhl)—a small pocket or sac in the skin from which hair or feathers grow

fossil—the hardened remains of an animal or plant that lived in a former time

hover—to hang fluttering or suspended in the air

humerus (HYOO-muhr-uhs)—in birds, the upper part of the wing from which the tertiaries grow

incubation (ihn-kyuh-BAY-shuhn)—the period before hatching during which the male or female bird will sit on the eggs to keep them warm

insulation—protection from heat and cold

iridescence (ir·uh·DEHS·uhns)—a play of colors producing rainbow effects

keratin (KAIR·uh·tihn)—the key element that makes up a feather

melanin (MEHL·uh·nihn)—a dark pigment found in the skin of humans and animals

microscopic (my·kroh·SKAHP·ihk)—an object so small that it cannot be seen without the aid of a microscope

migratory birds—birds that move from one area or climate to another for breeding or feeding

molting—the act of shedding fur or feathers before they are replaced with new growth

nibbling—a bird's method of preening or cleaning each feather individually using the tongue

ornithologists (ohr·nuh·THAHL·uh·jihsts)—scientists who study birds

papilla (puh·PIHL·uh)—a tiny knob at the root of a hair or feather

partial molt—the shedding of some feathers or fur

pigments—tiny "packages" of color found in the tissues of animals, plants, and people

plumage (PLOO·mihj)—the feathers of a bird

powder down—a fine powder that results from the wearing away of the down feathers; used for preening

predators (PREHD·uh·tuhrz)—animals that hunt other animals for food

preening—cleaning and straightening feathers using the beak

primaries—the long flight feathers of the wing

protective coloration—seasonal changes in coloring that serve as camouflage to protect the bird from predators

quill—the lowest part of the feather's shaft

rachis (RAY·kihs)—the upper part of the shaft of a feather

rudder—an instrument for steering; the tail of a bird used to steer in flight

secondaries—some of the flight feathers on the forearm of a bird's wing

shaft—the stiff, central rib of a feather

species (SPEE·sheez)—distinct kinds of animals or plants having common characteristics and a common name

tertiaries (TUR·shee·ehr·eez)—the smallest of the flight feathers on a bird

tracts—pathways on a bird's skin where feathers grow

tufts—clusters of feathers usually found on a bird's head

vane—the flat section of a feather composed of barbs

web—another name for vane

Index

About the Author

Karen O'Connor is the author of more than twenty books for young readers and more than three hundred articles and stories for adult and juvenile publications. Three of her books were named Outstanding Science Trade Books for Children. A former elementary school teacher, Ms. O'Connor currently works as a free-lance author, seminar leader, and writing instructor. She is a longtime member of the American Society of Journalists and Authors and the Society of Children's Book Writers. As a resident of San Diego, she enjoys bird watching year round.